U.S.NRC

United States Nuclear Regulatory Commission

Protecting People and the Environment

Protecting Our Nation

A Report of the U.S. Nuclear Regulatory Commission

Office of Nuclear Security and Incident Response

ACKNOWLEDGMENTS

Shyrl Coker

Sarah Loh

Rebecca Richardson

Jeffrey Riley

Rebecca Stone

TABLE OF CONTENTS

FOREWORD FROM THE CHAIRMAN

Since 2004, the U.S. Nuclear Regulatory Commission (NRC) has published and periodically updated "Protecting Our Nation" to provide an overview of the various ways in which the NRC protects our nation's civilian nuclear facilities from harm and works to ensure that radioactive material does not fall into the wrong hands. We are pleased to provide this updated edition to continue to share this important information with the public.

Chairman Allison M. Macfarlane speaks during the Regulatory Information Conference at NRC Headquarters.

Since the last edition, published two years ago, the NRC has continued its strong commitment to nuclear security. Recent changes to some of the NRC's security regulations will further strengthen our already rigorous program. We are also focusing significant attention on cyber security. The NRC recently developed and issued a cyber security roadmap to evaluate the need for cyber security requirements for fuel cycle facilities, nonpower reactors, Independent Spent Fuel Storage Installations (ISFSIs) and byproduct materials licensees. In January 2013, the NRC began conducting inspections of power reactor licensees' cyber security plans and implementation.

The NRC is also working cooperatively with its international regulatory counterparts to share best practices and lessons learned. In December 2012, the NRC hosted the first-ever International Security Regulators Conference with the objective of deepening our relationships with security regulators around the world. In addition, our extensive cooperation with the International Atomic Energy Agency (IAEA) helps ensure that our program benefits from international insights, and vice versa. The NRC hosted an IAEA International Physical Protection Advisory Service mission in an effort to seek further feedback on some aspects of our security program from the international community.

As many of you are aware, one important component of the NRC's security program is emergency preparedness and response. The 2011 Fukushima Daiichi accident reinforced the need for nuclear regulators to prepare themselves and their licensees to handle all kinds of emergencies, irrespective of their cause. At a nuclear site, safety and security systems are inherently integrated. The NRC is overseeing licensees' enhancements to their emergency communication and staffing plans as part of its effort to implement lessons learned from this accident. In addition, we continue to work diligently with our licensees and Federal, State, Tribal and local government officials in conducting safety- and security-focused drills and exercises. Our consistent attention to emergency preparedness and enhanced coordination with responsible organizations helps ensure that the NRC and its licensees would respond effectively to a variety of scenarios.

The tragedy of the September 11, 2001, terrorist attacks left an indelible imprint on our memory and served as the catalyst for lasting enhancements to the NRC's security program. Drawing upon this, we must be prepared to address threats from a variety of adversaries. We don't need to look further than the daily newspaper to see that both are constantly evolving. In this publication, you will learn about the many ways in which the NRC and its licensees work together to maintain a robust security program that protects some of our nation's most sensitive assets.

Allison Macfarlane

Chairman, NRC

EXECUTIVE SUMMARY

For over 35 years, the NRC has maintained effective nuclear security, emergency preparedness, and incident response programs as part of its mission to ensure adequate protection of public health and safety, to promote the common defense and security, and to protect the environment. The NRC requires safe and secure operations at all nuclear facilities. Generally, safety refers to operating the facility in a manner that protects the public and the environment, while security refers to protecting the facility from adversaries who wish to harm people and the environment. Safety and security are achieved by employing people, programs, and equipment to ensure implementation of robust programs as required by NRC regulations.

Security, like safety, is achieved in layers, with multiple approaches at work to provide high assurance that licensed activities do not cause unreasonable risk to public health and safety. For example, nuclear power plants are secure, robust structures that are designed and built to withstand hurricanes, tornadoes, and earthquakes. In addition, well-trained and armed security officers, physical barriers, access controls, and intrusion detection and surveillance systems are used to protect certain NRC-licensed facilities, such as commercial power reactors.

An additional layer of protection is in place related to coordinating threat information and response. The NRC works closely with Federal, State, Tribal, and local authorities. These relationships help ensure that the NRC can act quickly to disseminate threat information to licensees and allow effective emergency response in the event of an attack. Together, these layers of defense provide a level of security second to none in the Nation's commercial sector.

The NRC regulates mature, robust, and integrated security, emergency preparedness, and incident response programs at licensed facilities. This includes the development of new programs to address new and changing real world threats, as well as future challenges.

Among the topics covered in this document, the following major activities highlight recent NRC accomplishments:

- continued to verify that licensees have implemented security regulations through licensing reviews and inspections

- continued to use a high level of realism in force-on-force mock attack exercises while ensuring the safety of plant employees and the public and continually applying lessons learned from previous years

- continued to verify that licensees have implemented cyber security requirements

- continued efforts to safely and securely transport spent fuel along NRC approved routes using NRC-approved packages

- continued to implement the National Source Tracking System (NSTS) database, which enhances accountability for certain radioactive materials and requires licensees to report the manufacture, transfer, receipt, disassembly, and disposal of nationally tracked radioactive sources

- enhanced physical security requirements for radioactive materials and devices at facilities and in transportation

- assessed and shared threat information rapidly to promote protection of licensed facilities

- continued to support the development of international standards

- coordinated activities related to the nuclear industry's efforts to conduct emergency preparedness exercises initiated by hostile actions and prepared the industry and offsite response organizations for implementing hostile-action-based exercises

- ensured continuous training and improvement to equipment and procedures in the NRC Headquarters Operations Center (HOC) and regional Incident Response Centers

Executive Director for Operations, Mark A. Satorius speaks to NRC stakeholders.

SECURITY AT NUCLEAR REACTORS

Security for Operating, New, and Nonpower Reactors

The NRC requires robust security at the Nation's nuclear facilities. Effective NRC regulation, licensee implementation of these regulations, and strong partnerships with a variety of Federal, State, Tribal, and local authorities have ensured effective security at operating power reactors across the country. In fact, nuclear plants are possibly the best protected industrial facilities in the United States. However, given the current threat environment, the agency recognizes the need for continued vigilance.

An NRC-licensed operating nuclear power plant.

The NRC's operating power reactor security baseline inspection program is the primary way in which the agency verifies that nuclear power plants operate according to security regulations. Force-on-force security inspec-

tions are one of the most significant components of the NRC's baseline security inspection program. Force-on-force inspections assess the ability of these facilities to defend against the Design Basis Threat (DBT) for radiological sabotage[1] and provide valuable insights that enable the NRC to evaluate and improve the effectiveness of licensees' security programs.

U.S. Operating Commercial Nuclear Power Reactors

Infographic map of the U.S. operating commercial nuclear power reactors displayed by the four NRC regions.

This DBT describes the adversary force that operating power reactors must defend against with high assurance. It is based on realistic assessments of the tactics, techniques, and procedures used by international and domestic terrorist groups and organizations. Additionally, the NRC has comprehensive security regulations for operating power reactors that include a cyber security threat component to the DBT. All power reactor licensees have developed cyber security plans which the NRC has reviewed and approved. The NRC conducts inspections to verify that operating power reactor licensees are implementing cyber security requirements.

On an ongoing basis, the NRC ensures that the security posture at operating power reactors is appropriate, including any changes or updates to security plans or procedures, and that they provide a high assurance of protection against the DBT. As with other categories of licensees, this is accomplished through a wide spectrum of licensing, inspection, and enforcement activities.

An NRC Resident Inspector for a nuclear power plant construction site, explains the inspection activities.

Additionally, 4 new nuclear power plants are currently under construction. In recent years, the NRC has received a number of applications for new reactors and expects to receive more in the future. As the Nation's civilian nuclear regulator, the NRC has many programs in place to meet the challenges associated with new nuclear power plant construction. These "next-generation" nuclear plant designs have benefited from the decades of experience gained from current operating plants. The new designs are inherently safer and more secure. They will use many passive systems, further ensuring safety with limited reactor operator action.

A containment vessel under construction at a nuclear power plant site.

NRC regulations require applicants for new reactor design approvals and construction to perform a design-specific assessment of the effects of the impact of a large commercial aircraft. New Reactors will have inherent protection against aircraft impact.

The physical location of each new nuclear power plant is also closely analyzed. The U.S. Department of Homeland Security (DHS) has the authority and responsibility for a

---

[1] Radiological sabotage is a determined violent external assault, attack by stealth, or deceptive actions, including diversionary actions, by an adversary force capable of operating in each of the following modes: a single group attacking through one entry point, multiple groups attacking through multiple entry points, a combination of one or more groups and one or more individuals attacking through multiple entry points, or individuals attacking through separate entry points, with attributes, assistance and equipment as described in Title 10 of the Code of Federal Regulations (10 CFR) Part 73 "Physical Protection of Plants and Materials."

unified National effort to secure the United States by preventing, deterring, and responding to terrorist attacks and other threats and hazards to the Nation. Therefore, the NRC consults with DHS about the potential vulnerabilities of a proposed facility's location to a terrorist threat.

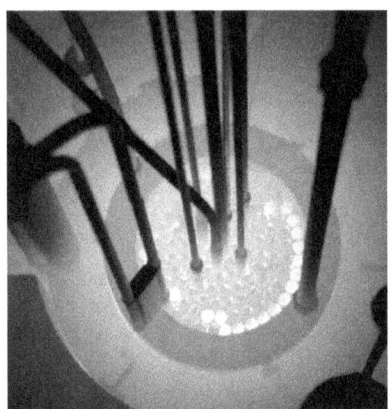

The NRC regulates 32 Nonpower Reactors nationwide.

Nonpower reactors (NPRs), on the other hand, pose significantly less risk of radiological exposure to the public than do power reactors. Consequently, the NRC has tailored the security requirements and oversight for NPRs to be consistent with these lower risks. The NRC works with the NPR community to improve security by identifying any potential vulnerabilities that warrant additional preventive or mitigating measures.

The NRC considers the following two main elements in establishing additional security measures for NPRs:

(1)   The low potential radiological consequences make it unlikely that a terrorist attack could compromise public health and safety.

(2)   Each licensee implements site specific security plans because each NPR facility is unique in design, operation, use, and location.

The NRC also works with licensees and the U.S. Department of Energy (DOE) to evaluate steps to reduce the inventories of reactor fuel at NPRs. This includes converting those reactors using highly-enriched uranium to using low enriched uranium through the DOE's Global Threat Reduction Initiative.

Design Basis Threat for Radiological Sabotage

The DBT for radiological sabotage describes the adversary force that operating power reactors must defend against with high assurance. It is based on realistic assessments of the tactics, techniques, and procedures used by international and domestic terrorist groups and organizations. This DBT is developed by working with national experts and is based on classified and other sensitive information. The NRC also relies on the intelligence community, law enforcement agencies, and State and local governments to provide accurate and timely information about the capabilities and activities of adversary groups.

It is the responsibility of other Federal organizations, including the military, to protect the Nation against airborne threats. Nonetheless, the NRC has conducted several comprehensive studies that determined that an aircraft impact is unlikely to result in damage to the core or a radiological release. In its requirements for operating power reactors, the NRC also requires its licensees to take steps to mitigate the effects of large fires and explosions from any type of initiating event. The NRC is an active partner with other Federal, State, and local authorities in constant surveillance of the airborne threat environment and adjusts its regulatory actions or requirements, as necessary.

Barriers are part of the physical protection system used by operating reactors to defend against the DBT.

The NRC staff regularly reviews this DBT against the current threat intelligence, both domestic and interna-

tional, to determine if any changes are warranted. Specific characteristics of this DBT are not publicly available in order to protect sensitive security information that could potentially aid an adversary.

Barriers are part of the physical protection system used by operating reactors to defend against the DBT.

In general, this DBT determines how operating power reactors establish their:

- cyber security program

- security patrols

- security posts and physical barriers

- vehicle inspections and the appropriate standoff distance

- training for security and emergency response personnel

- enhanced weapons systems needed to implement an effective strategy

- types and numbers of communication equipment

- site access controls for personnel, including more thorough employee background checks

Security Baseline Inspections

The NRC's operating power reactor security baseline inspection program is the primary method in which the agency verifies that nuclear power plants operate according to security regulations. Under the program, security experts from NRC Headquarters and Regional offices in the Philadelphia, Atlanta, Chicago, and Dallas areas carry out security inspections at each facility. On-site Resident Inspectors, in conjunction with inspectors from Headquarters and the Regional offices, monitor licensees' security-related activities throughout the year. The inspectors provide firsthand, independent assessments of plant conditions and performance, document their findings in writing, and conduct follow-up inspections to ensure that the licensee has made any necessary corrections.

An NRC inspector gathers information at a nuclear power plant.

Security baseline inspections include the following licensee activities:

- Access Authorization

- Access Control

- Contingency Response Force-on-Force

- Equipment Performance, Testing, and Maintenance

- Protective Strategy Evaluation

- Protection of Safeguards Information (SGI)

- Security Training

- Fitness-for-Duty Program

- Cyber Security

- Materials Control and Accounting

- Target Set Development

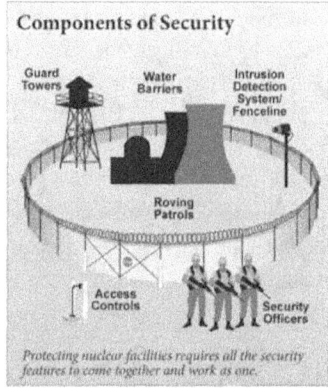

The NRC's overall evaluation of an operating power reactor's performance considers the results of security inspections. However, if a significant security issue is found, the NRC requires the licensee to resolve the issue promptly. If necessary, the NRC can take enforcement action which may result in civil penalties. Some information related to these inspections is available to the public via the NRC website. However, some of the information is not publicly available in order to protect sensitive security information that could potentially aid an adversary.

Force-on-Force Security Inspections

Force-on-force security inspections are one of the components of the NRC's security baseline inspection program. The NRC has used force-on-force inspections regularly as part of its inspection process since 1991. Force-on-force inspections assess the ability of power reactor facilities to defend against the DBT for radiological sabotage and provide valuable insights that enable the NRC to evaluate the effectiveness of licensee security programs. They are an essential part of the oversight of the security of these facilities.

An adversary force approaches a nuclear power plant during a force-on-force training exercise.

A full force-on-force inspection spans several weeks. It includes both tabletop drills and simulated combat between a mock adversary force and the operating power reactor's force. During the inspection, the mock adversary force attempts to reach and damage key safety systems and components identified as target sets while battling the plant's security force. These key safety systems and components protect the reactor

core and the spent nuclear fuel pool, both of which may contain radioactive fuel. For that reason, it is essential to protect these systems and components from being reached by the adversary force to avoid the potential for radiological release.

Along with the facility's security personnel, many offsite organizations may participate in and/or observe force-on-force inspections. These organizations include Federal, State, and local law enforcement agencies. In addition, emergency planning officials, plant operators, and NRC personnel are present.

By law, the NRC conducts a force-on-force inspection at each plant at least once every 3 years. The NRC uses lessons learned from previous force-on-force inspections in making changes to its procedures and inspector training programs.

The force-on-force program ensures a high level of realism during the inspection, while ensuring the safety of operating nuclear reactor employees and the public. The force-on-force inspection involves two shifts of the licensee's security officers: one set maintains the plant's security, while the other set participates in the inspection. In addition, a separate group controls and monitors both inspection participants and on-duty security officers during the inspection. The NRC has overall control of the exercise and the NRC inspection team monitors all aspects of the exercise activities to ensure the safety of the participants and the conduct of the exercise in accordance with approved NRC inspection standards. In preparation for a force-on-force inspection, participants compile information from tabletop drills, other inspections, and security plan reviews. This information is then used to design a number of mock attacks seeking to probe for potential vulnerabilities in the defensive strategy used at a specific operating power reactor. Any potentially significant findings identified during a force-on-force inspection are promptly reviewed, addressed, and corrected before the NRC inspectors leave the plant.

Active-duty U.S. Special Operations Forces advise the NRC inspection teams that conduct force-on-force inspections. These individuals participate in the inspections by helping the NRC inspectors develop the attack scenarios, providing expert technical advice to the mock adversary force, assisting the NRC inspectors in evaluating site security forces and systems, and providing an independent evaluation of mock adversary performance.

The adversary is a credible, well trained, and consistent mock force that is vital to the NRC's force-on-force program. The NRC works with the nuclear industry to develop mock adversary training and uses rigorous performance standards to evaluate the mock adversary force at each inspection.

NRC Chairman Allison M. Macfarlane listens to staff discuss security topics at the International Regulators Conference on Nuclear Security at NRC Headquarters.

It is important to emphasize that the NRC designs, runs, and evaluates the force-on-force inspections. The mock adversary force does not establish the inspection's objectives, boundaries, or timelines. To date, the performance of the mock adversary force has been exceptional, and no instances of a possible conflict of interest have been identified.

MATERIALS SECURITY

Security for the Use, Storage, and Transportation of Nuclear and Radiological Materials

The NRC has longstanding regulatory programs to ensure the security of materials that it licenses. Nuclear materials are used to produce fuel for nuclear reactors and can be the primary ingredients for an improvised nuclear device. The NRC requires licensees to apply a graded level of physical protection and material control and accounting, depending on the material and the relative potential consequences if it is misused. Security programs may include background checks, personnel access controls, security barriers, detection of unauthorized access, and an armed law enforcement response. These programs provide the greatest protection to those materials that could be used in harmful ways if not protected. Given the current threat environment, the agency recognizes the need for continued vigilance.

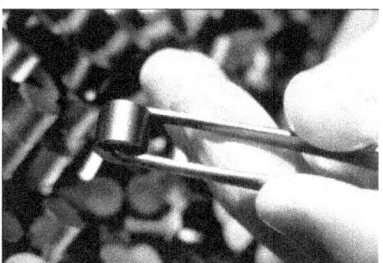

A small ceramic fuel pellet.

The NRC licenses and inspects all commercial fuel cycle facilities that turn uranium ore from the ground into fuel for nuclear reactors. This includes uranium recovery facilities that mill uranium; facilities that convert, enrich, and fabricate the uranium into nuclear fuel for use in nuclear reactors; and deconversion facilities that will process the depleted uranium hexafluoride for recycling or disposal.

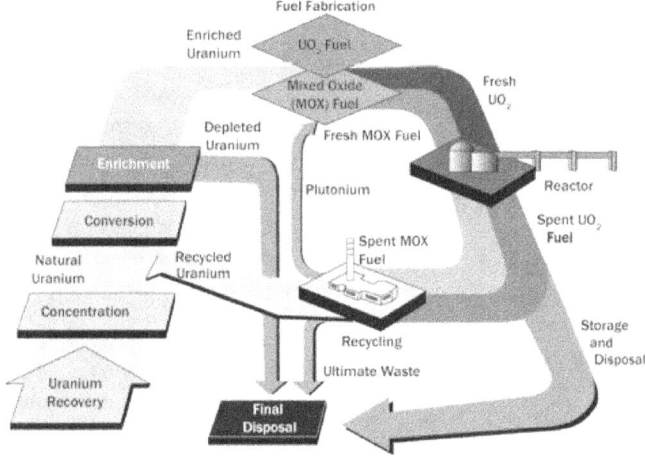

The stages of the nuclear fuel cycle.

The NRC also regulates the fabrication of other types of nuclear fuel, such as mixed oxide fuel, which is a combination of uranium and plutonium oxides.

The NRC regulates fuel cycle facilities through a combination of the following:

- safety and security regulations that licensees must meet to obtain and retain a license to use nuclear materials

- authorization for an applicant to use or transport nuclear materials or operate a nuclear facility

- an oversight process that includes inspections, enforcement, assessment of licensee performance, and investigation of reports of wrongdoing

- support activities (e.g., research, hearings, independent reviews)

Additionally, the NRC has issued orders to various fuel cycle facilities containing detailed requirements related to detection of, assessment of, and response to malicious acts, including enhancing the protection of their computer systems. In 2012, the NRC developed and issued a cyber security paper that communicates the staff's approach, or roadmap, to evaluate the need for cyber security requirements for specific types of licensees, including fuel cycle facilities. The roadmap is designed to ensure that appropriate cyber security protections are implemented efficiently at all NRC-licensed fuel cycle facilities. The purpose of these regulatory actions is to ensure adequate protection of public health and safety, promote the common defense and security, and to protect the environment for licensed activities at fuel facilities.

The NRC imposes stringent requirements to ensure the safe and secure operation of spent fuel pools.

Spent nuclear fuel refers to fuel from nuclear reactors that is no longer being used. Periodically, approximately one third of the nuclear fuel in an operating reactor needs to be replaced with fresh fuel. Spent nuclear fuel is safely stored in specially designed pools at reactor sites around the country. Spent fuel pools are robust structures constructed of very thick steel-reinforced concrete walls with stainless steel liners located inside protected areas at nuclear power reactor sites. Many fuel pools are located below ground level, are shielded by other structures, and have intervening walls that would obstruct something that could make a large impact, such as an aircraft. The NRC regulations require licensees to develop guidance and strategies to maintain and restore spent fuel pool cooling using existing or available resources if cooling is lost.

For many events, plant operators would have significant time to correct a problem or implement fixes to restore cooling.

The NRC has also authorized nuclear power plant licensees to store spent nuclear fuel at current and former reactor sites in NRC-approved dry storage casks. Beginning in the 1980s, the nuclear industry began storing spent nuclear fuel on site in storage casks located at ISFSIs. These casks are robust, massive concrete and steel structures and provide additional space for sites with limited space in their spent fuel pools. The NRC conducted security vulnerability assessments of several cask designs used at dry storage ISFSIs. These assessments included aircraft impacts and ground assaults consistent with the DBT. The NRC has always required ISFSIs to have an onsite physical security system to protect against any unauthorized access to the spent nuclear fuel and its storage area.

Independent spent fuel storage installations store spent fuel safely and securely.

The NRC is updating regulations to improve the consistency and clarity of the security measures for ISFSIs.

The NRC encourages members of the public and other stakeholders to provide comments during the development of the updated regulations. In addition, the NRC continues to evaluate whether changes in adversary capabilities could significantly affect ISFSI security. The NRC is engaging with other Government agencies, intelligence and law enforcement communities, and national laboratories in this task.

A radiography camera and its approved transport container.

Nuclear and radioactive materials are also used in many beneficial ways in the areas of medicine, academia, and industry; however, some materials if misused can have negative effects on people and the environment. The terrorist attacks on September 11, 2001, heightened concerns about the use of risk-significant radioactive materials in a malevolent act. Such materials could be used in a "dirty bomb".

After September 11, 2001, the NRC and its partners in Agreement States took steps to strengthen the security of risk-significant radioactive materials. The NRC and Agreement States issued various orders imposing comprehensive security measures that are appropriate to the facilities housing the materials and the level of security risk posed by the materials.

The security orders established a multi-layered, non-prescriptive framework that allows licensees to develop security programs specifically tailored to their facilities.

Key elements of the program include:

- Background checks, including fingerprinting, to ensure that people with access to radioactive material are trustworthy and reliable

- Personnel access controls to areas where radioactive material is stored or used

- Security plans or procedures designed to detect, deter, assess and respond to unauthorized access attempts

- Coordination and response planning between licensees and local law enforcement agencies

- Coordination and tracking of shipments of radioactive material

- Additional security barriers to discourage theft of portable devices containing radioactive material

In 2013, the NRC published security regulations in a new comprehensive rule titled, Part 37, "Physical Protection of Byproduct Material". The Part 37 rule incorporates and expands upon the requirements from the security orders and includes lessons learned from implementing, inspecting and enforcing the orders. Compliance with Part 37 will be required for NRC licensees by March 2014. The Agreement States must publish compatible regulations by March 2016. The security orders will remain in effect until the rule is implemented.

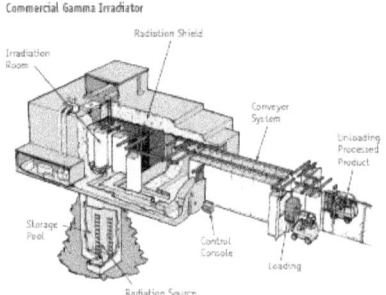
Commercial Gamma Irradiator

Additionally, the NRC developed an Integrated Source Management Portfolio. It includes the National Source Tracking System (NSTS), the Web-Based Licensing (WBL) database, and the License Verification System (LVS). The NSTS is a database that enhances accountability for certain radioactive sources that pose the greatest safety and security concerns. The NSTS requires licensees to report the manufacture, transfer, receipt, disassembly, and disposal of radioactive sources that are required to be tracked nationally. The NSTS is an important component of the NRC's effort to enhance the accountability and security of radioactive sources. WBL, a second database, was implemented in 2012.

This system manages the licensing lifecycle from initial application to license issuance, amendment, and termination. It also modernizes the method for authenticating radioactive material licenses. The NRC uses WBL as its licensing system, and it is available to Agreement States for their licensing purposes. Another important system was added in 2013 – the LVS. LVS provides a secure, fast, digital system that permits licensees to confirm that another party is properly licensed and authorized to possess radioactive material before shipping or transferring radioactive material to that party.

NRC requires robust security measures when spent nuclear fuel or significant quantities of radioactive material are transported.

The NRC regulates the transportation of nuclear and radiological materials through a combination of safety and security requirements. About 300 million shipments of hazardous material are transported by road, rail, or water in the United States each year. Of those shipments, only about 3 million involve radioactive material, most of which is low-level radioactive material. Fewer than 50 shipments contain spent nuclear fuel from nuclear power plants. Spent nuclear fuel has been successfully transported in NRC-approved containers safely and securely since 1979.

The NRC requires licensees and carriers involved in spent nuclear fuel shipments to follow approved routes.

For decades, the NRC has required radioactive material containers to withstand different types of accidents, including dropping, puncturing, flooding, and fire. Security measures complement these safety controls. For example, the NRC requires licensees and carriers involved in spent nuclear fuel shipments to follow approved routes and to provide armed escorts, vehicle immobilization devices, and redundant communications. The licensees notify the NRC and States the transport will pass through in advance of the shipments.

For more than 30 years, spent nuclear fuel has been transported under stringent security requirements. After September 11, 2001, the NRC reviewed its transportation security program. Following that review, the NRC required security enhancements for both shipments of spent nuclear fuel and shipments of significant quantities of radioactive material.

These enhancements include the following:

- preplanning, coordination, and advance notice of shipments

- additional monitoring of shipments

- verification of the trustworthiness of people with information about the shipments

The NRC also adjusted the security measures for shipments to reflect changes in the DHS National Terrorism Advisory System regarding the current threat level. During periods of heightened security, the NRC can issue specific advisories to enhance security. These advisories include suspending spent nuclear fuel shipments and requesting that licensees defer shipments of significant quantities of radioactive material.

Effective NRC regulation, licensee implementation of these regulations, and strong partnerships with a variety of Federal, State, Tribal, and local authorities have ensured effective security for the storage and transportation of nuclear and radiological materials across the country.

Design Basis Threat for Theft or Diversion[2]

The DBT for theft or diversion describes the adversary force that Category I[3] fuel cycle facilities must defend against. Additionally, these facilities must defend against the DBT for

radiological sabotage, as discussed on page 8. Similar to the DBT for radiological sabotage, the DBT for theft or diversion is based on realistic assessments of the tactics, techniques, and procedures used by international and domestic terrorist groups and organizations. The NRC also relies on the intelligence community, law enforcement agencies, and State and local governments to provide accurate and timely information about the capabilities and activities of adversary groups.

Security barriers provide one of the many layers of physical protection.

Following September 11, 2001, the NRC thoroughly reviewed both DBTs to ensure that Category I fuel cycle facilities continued to have effective security measures in place that account for the evolving threat environment. The NRC issued orders that upgraded the DBTs as a result of this review. These orders were later incorporated in a revised DBT rule. The rule reflects insights gained from the latest threat information and includes a cyber threat component.

---

[2] Theft or diversion of formula quantities of strategic special nuclear material is a determined violent external assault, attack by stealth, or deceptive actions, including diversionary actions, by an adversary force capable of operating in each of the following modes: a single group attacking through one entry point, multiple groups attacking through one or more groups and one or individuals attacking through multiple entry points, or individuals attacking through separate entry points, with attributes, assistance and equipment as described in Title 10 of the Code of Federal Regulations (10 CFR) Part 73 "Physical Protection of Plants and Materials."

[3] Fuel cycle facilities that possess more than 5,000 grams (about 11 pounds) of strategic special nuclear material (defined as a "formula quantity") or more as computed by the formula, grams = (grams contained U-235) + 2.5 (grams U-233 + grams plutonium) as further described in 10 CFR Part 73 "Physical Protection of Plants and Materials."

Vehicle barriers are part of the physical protection system used by some nuclear facilities.

The agency also considered, and as appropriate, incorporated the following 12 factors identified in the Energy Policy Act of 2005:

1) The events of September 11, 2001

2) An assessment of physical, cyber, biochemical, and other terrorist threats

3) The potential for attack on facilities by multiple coordinated teams of a large number of individuals

4) The potential for assistance in an attack from several persons employed at the facility;

5) The potential for suicide attacks

6) The potential for water-based and air-based threats

7) The potential use of explosive devices of considerable size and other modern weaponry

8) The potential for attacks by persons with a sophisticated knowledge of facility operations

9) The potential for fires, especially fires of long duration

10) The potential for attacks on spent fuel shipments by multiple coordinated teams of a large number of individuals

11) The adequacy of planning to protect the public health and safety at and around nuclear facilities, as appropriate, in the event of a terrorist attack against a nuclear facility

12) The potential for theft or diversion of nuclear material from such facilities

The NRC regularly reviews the DBTs against the current threat intelligence, both domestic and international, to determine whether any changes are warranted. Specific characteristics of the DBTs are not publicly available in order to protect sensitive security information that could potentially aid an adversary.

NRC licensees have measures that limit the exposure of security personnel to possible attack, including the incorporation of bullet-resisting protected positions that provide protection against the DBT.

Security Core Inspections

The NRC's security core inspection program is the primary way in which the agency ensures the physical protection of fuel cycle facilities and transport of certain nuclear material according to security regulations. Under the program, security experts (primarily from NRC Headquarters and the regional office in Atlanta) carry out security inspections.

The experts provide firsthand, independent assessments of site conditions and performance, document their findings in writing, and conduct follow-up inspections to ensure that the licensee has made any necessary corrections.

An NRC inspector gathers information at an NRC facility.

Resident inspectors, in conjunction with inspectors from Headquarters and the Region, monitor licensees' security-related activities on a daily basis throughout the year. Security core inspections may include the following inspectable areas:

- Access Authorization
- Access Control
- Contingency Response Force-on-Force
- Equipment Performance, Testing, and Maintenance
- Protective Strategy Evaluation
- Protection of Classified and Safeguards Information
- Security Training
- Fitness-for-Duty Program
- Cyber Security
- Target Area Review
- Transportation Security

The NRC's overall evaluation of licensee performance considers the results of security inspections. However, if a significant security issue is found, the NRC requires the licensee to resolve the issue promptly. If necessary, the NRC can take enforcement action that includes civil penalties. Some information related to these inspections is available to the public via the NRC website. However, much of the information is not publicly available in order to protect sensitive security information that could potentially aid an adversary.

Perimeter Intrusion & Delay Time

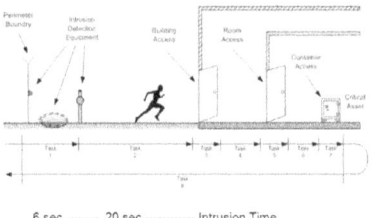

6 sec -------- 20 sec ------------ Intrusion Time

Force-on-Force Security Inspections

Force-on-force security inspections are one of the components of the NRC's security core inspection program at fuel cycle facilities. Force-on-force inspections assess the ability of these facilities to defend against the DBT for theft or diversion and provide valuable insights that enable the NRC to evaluate and improve the effectiveness of the security programs at Category I fuel cycle facilities. They are an essential part of the oversight of the security of these facilities. The fuel cycle facility force-on-force program uses the same processes and many of the same staff as performed at power reactors.

Two members of the adversary force simulate a breach of the Protected Area at a site during a training exercise.

As with power reactor programs, full force-on-force inspection spans several weeks. It includes both tabletop drills and simulated combat between a mock adversary force and the nuclear facility's security force. During the inspection, the mock adversary force attempts to reach Target Areas while battling the site's security force. Target Areas require protection from malicious actions such as theft or diversion. For that reason, it is essential to protect these systems and components from being reached by the adversary force.

Along with the facility's security personnel, many offsite organizations may participate in and observe force-on-force inspections. These organizations include Federal, State, and local law enforcement agencies. In addition, emergency planning officials, site operators, and NRC personnel are present.

By law, the NRC conducts a force-on-force inspection at least once every 3 years. The NRC uses lessons learned from previous force-on-force inspections in making changes to its procedures and inspector training programs.

The force-on-force program ensures a high level of realism during the inspection, while ensuring the safety of site employees and the public. The force-on-force inspection involves two sets of the licensee's security officers. One set maintains the site's security, while the other set participates in the inspection. In addition, a separate group controls and monitors both inspection participants and on-duty security officers during the inspection. The NRC has overall control of the exercise and the NRC inspection team monitors all aspects of the exercise activities to ensure the safety of the participants and the conduct of the exercise in accordance with approved inspection standards.

In force-on-force inspections, the use of weapons and explosives can be simulated using electronic equipment.

In preparation for a force-on-force inspection, participants compile information from tabletop drills, other inspections, and security plan reviews. This information is then used to design a number of mock attacks seeking to probe for potential deficiencies in the defensive strategy used at a specific site. Any potentially significant findings identified during a force-on-force inspection are promptly reviewed, addressed, and corrected before the NRC inspectors leave the site.

Active-duty U.S. Special Operations Forces advise the NRC inspection teams that conduct force-on-force inspections. These individuals participate in the inspections by helping the NRC inspectors develop the scenarios, providing expert technical advice to the mock adversary force, and assisting the NRC inspectors in evaluating site security forces and systems. It is important to emphasize that the NRC designs, runs, and evaluates the force-on-force inspections. The mock adversary force does not establish the inspection objectives, boundaries, or timelines.

CYBER SECURITY

Establishing and maintaining effective cyber security is a growing challenge across the Nation. New domestic and international adversaries are emerging, as are new tools that these adversaries can use to exploit potentially vulnerable systems and their supply chains. Historically, digital computer systems played a limited role in the operation of nuclear facilities. However, digital systems are increasingly being used to help maximize plant productivity. Computer systems that monitor and control operating nuclear reactors' safety systems and that help the plants operate are isolated from external communications, including the Internet, to protect against outside intrusion. The NRC is working with its Federal partners to address the complicated issue of cyber security.

Following September 11, 2001, the NRC issued a series of advisories and orders requiring nuclear facilities to take certain actions, including enhancing the protection of their computer systems. Since that time, the NRC has replaced those interim measures with comprehensive regulations for operating power reactors and added a cyber security threat component to both DBTs. Systems covered by the regulations include systems associated with those related to safety, important to safety, security, and emergency preparedness functions, and those support systems and equipment that, if compromised, could adversely impact safety, important to safety, security, and emergency preparedness functions. The NRC also published regulatory guidance for cyber security that provides an acceptable approach for protecting digital computers, communications systems, and networks from a cyber attack. All operating power reactor licensees have developed cyber security plans that the NRC has reviewed and approved. The NRC is conducting inspections to ensure that operating power reactor licensees are implementing cyber security requirements.

Recent high-profile cyber attacks on critical infrastructure sectors underscore the importance of evaluating cyber security requirements for all classes of NRC licensees. The experience with operating power reactors has helped the agency develop new requirements promptly and effectively. In 2012, the NRC developed and issued a cyber security paper that communicates the staff's approach,

or roadmap, to evaluate the need for cyber security requirements for fuel cycle facilities, NPRs, ISFSIs, and byproduct materials licensees. The implementation of this roadmap will ensure that appropriate levels of cyber security actions are implemented in a timely and efficient manner at all NRC-licensed facilities and will identify whether any program improvements are needed.

In addition, the agency established a new internal organizational component, the Cyber Security Directorate (CSD), in 2013 that plans, coordinates, and manages agency-wide activities related to cyber security for NRC licensees. The CSD is responsible for rulemaking, guidance, licensing, policy issues, and oversight related to cyber security requirements. Within the CSD is a cyber assessment team that assesses real world cyber events at NRC-licensed facilities. The team evaluates whether an identified threat could impact licensed facilities and makes recommendations for NRC actions and communications to the licensees.

NUCLEAR PREPAREDNESS AND RESPONSE

Emergency Preparedness

For over 35 years, the NRC has provided regulatory oversight for emergency planning and incident response for all of its licensees. Commercial nuclear power plants are required to conduct a full scale exercise involving Federal, State, Tribal, and local agencies at least once every 2 years. The NRC and the Federal Emergency Management Agency (FEMA) evaluate these exercises to verify that emergency preparedness programs and the skills of the emergency responders remain effective and identify any weaknesses. The NRC assesses the onsite response, whereas FEMA assesses the offsite response. In the years between evaluated exercises, licensees conduct various drills to test key functions and maintain emergency responder skills.

Before 2001, only a few emergency preparedness exercises simulated hostile actions against a nuclear power plant as their full-scale exercise. A hostile action is an act that uses violent force in an attempt to destroy equipment, take hostages, or intimidate the licensee to achieve an end. Even though the potential radiological consequences would be the same whether caused by a hostile action or a safety event, hostile actions would likely pose unique challenges to emergency responders. Therefore, the NRC updated its regulations to require each site to conduct an evaluated hostile action-based (HAB) drill at least once every 8 years.

A team of NRC officials views a steel plate-covered spent fuel pool at the Fukushima Daiichi complex in Japan. Courtesy of TEPCO.

With respect to HAB exercises, the NRC requires nuclear power plant licensees to:

- identify alternate emergency response facilities located offsite to support the mobilization and staging of licensee emergency response organization personnel

- notify the NRC promptly for identified potential or actual hostile actions against the nuclear power plant site

- develop specific hostile action-based emergency action levels for the classification of emergencies

- establish new protective action strategies for onsite personnel in the event of a hostile action against the nuclear power plant site

These measures are tested through drills and exercises, and are continually verified by NRC inspectors.

The NRC has also conducted a formal review of each licensee's emergency preparedness planning basis to verify that it will adequately protect public health and safety in light of the current threat environment. The review concluded that emergency preparedness at nuclear power plants remains strong, but could be improved in such areas as communications, resource management, drill programs, and NRC guidance.

Many of these considerations and improvements have been incorporated as enhancements to emergency preparedness regulations.

Incident Response

The NRC responds to incidents associated with all of its licensed facilities and activities. In addition, the NRC regularly provides support to other Federal, State, and local response agencies during major events such as hurricanes, floods, and wildfires. The NRC coordinates its response actions with other agencies through the use of NRC guidance and in a manner consistent with the National Response Framework (NRF).

Chairman Allison M. Macfarlane discusses possible response measures with the members of the Executive Team during an Emergency Preparedness exercise.

Headquarters Operations Center

The NRC directs its response to events from the Headquarters Operations Center (HOC). The operations center is staffed 24 hours a day, 7 days a week, with 2 Headquarters Operations Officers who have the experience and knowledge to evaluate and respond properly to reported events. Their actions may include: informing NRC management; informing the agency's Federal partners, licensees, and the media; and potentially staffing the HOC at the necessary level based on the direction of senior management. Recently the HOC was upgraded to a new facility with advanced technology and improved equipment, which enhances the ability of the NRC to respond to events, including circumstances involving multiple facilities. NRC response capability is also improved through the continual training of qualified responders, training and qualification of new staff, and continuous reviews of policies, processes, and procedures of the response organization.

Staff at the NRC's Headquarters Operations Center monitor simulated plant conditions during an Emergency Preparedness exercise with a nuclear power plant.

An alternate incident response center exists to continue the work of the HOC in case the Headquarters facility is not available. Each of the NRC's four regional offices also has an incident response center, all of which have been recently upgraded to allow seamless transition of response duties in the event that any of the other response centers become unavailable.

Continuity of Operations

The NRC Continuity of Operations (COOP) plan ensures that the agency can continue to operate after a major event that disrupts normal operations. In recent years, the NRC has upgraded and tested its COOP capabilities and has participated in annual national-level COOP exercises. The NRC exercises its COOP capabilities to prepare for incidents that could disrupt normal operations. In addition, the COOP plan addresses agency functions in the event of a pandemic. The NRC's COOP plan is regularly reviewed and updated based on the lessons learned during exercises and real-world events.

Interagency Response

The NRC coordinates its activities with other Federal agencies to improve its response to both nuclear safety and security emergencies. Using the NRF, the NRC works with local, Tribal, State, and Federal agencies in both the prevention of and response to a nuclear safety or a hostile action event. The NRC has a proven history of providing resources to its partners during exercises and actual events and will continue to work with other Federal agencies to implement the NRF.

The National Infrastructure Protection Plan (NIPP), issued by DHS, also provides a framework for coordination and information sharing among Federal agencies, State and local governments, and private sector critical infrastructure protection stakeholders. The NIPP framework also facilitates a coordinated response to threats and events affecting the Nation's critical infrastructure by establishing roles and responsibilities of Federal, State, local, Tribal, and private sector critical infrastructure partners. Furthermore, the NIPP sets national priorities and goals for the effective distribution of funding and resources to help enhance the resilience of the U.S. Government, economy, and public services in the event of natural or man-made disasters.

The NRC actively supports FEMA's National Exercise Program. This program serves as the principal exercise mechanism for examining the preparedness and measuring the readiness of the United States by testing the Nation's ability to perform missions or functions that prevent, protect against, respond to, recover from, and mitigate all hazards. Thus, scenarios can be used that potentially involve simulated weapons of mass destruction, major storms, or terrorist attacks.

Participating in these exercises provides the NRC with valuable feedback to enhance its own response program.

Another example of interagency coordination is the DHS-led Comprehensive Review Program of commercial nuclear reactors and associated spent nuclear fuel storage facilities. This review identified strengths and potential areas for improvement in the Nation's critical infrastructure and key resources. The NRC continues to work with industry and DHS to ensure that progress is made in addressing any notable improvement areas.

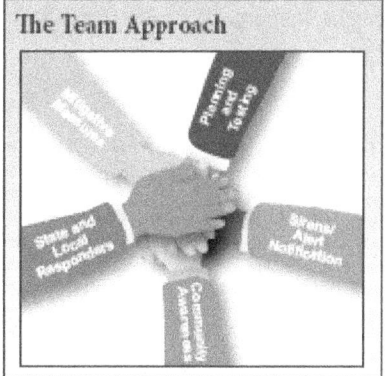

Effective preparedness and response requires cooperation among the Federal Government, State, and local officials, the public, and the NRC licensees.

ADDITIONAL SECURITY ACTIVITIES

Communications

An important part of protecting nuclear facilities from acts of terrorism is effective communication among the NRC, NRC-licensed facilities and certificate holders, and Federal, State, Tribal, Territorial, and local governments. The NRC continues to enhance its communications with upgrades, including a protected web-based computer server system to exchange sensitive security information quickly with licensees and authorized government officials. Using secure transmission equipment, the NRC can rapidly communicate classified and sensitive unclassified information among NRC Headquarters, regional offices, and licensees.

The NRC works with a variety of partners to fulfill its mission and maintains close working relationships with Congress and State officials. The NRC regularly communicates with Federal partners about policy and programs including the following:

- U.S. Department of Defense

- U.S. Department of Energy (DOE)

- DOE National Nuclear Security Administration

- U.S. Department of Homeland Security (DHS)

- DHS Federal Emergency Management Agency (FEMA)

NRC staff speak at a public meeting on security requirements at NRC-regulated facilities.

- DHS Transportation Security Administration

- DHS Domestic Nuclear Detection Office

- U.S. Department of State

- U.S. Department of Transportation

- Federal Aviation Administration

- Federal Bureau of Investigation (FBI)

- National Security Council

- North American Aerospace Defense Command (NORAD)

- U.S. Northern Command

- Office of the Director of National Intelligence

- National Counterterrorism Center

- Other members of the Intelligence Community

In addition, the NRC communicates directly with other Federal agencies about specific threats. For example, NORAD contacts the NRC directory to share information about potential aircraft threats against NRC regulated nuclear facilities. This communication and coordination lays the foundation for ongoing national efforts to detect, prevent, and respond to terrorist attacks.

The NRC continues to explore areas in which sharing information will result in a better-informed and better-prepared Nation. However, the agency must prevent unauthorized individuals or those without a need-to-know from gaining access to sensitive information that might compromise security at NRC regulated facilities. As a result, the NRC must balance its commitment to openness with the need to prevent the release of sensitive information.

Information Security

The NRC's information security program protects classified Restricted Data (RD) and National Security Information (NSI), SGI, and other sensitive information from unauthorized disclosure. Only those with the appropriate security clearance and a need-to-know can view such information. The NRC requires security clearances for appropriate individuals at NRC regulated facilities. These clearances provide licensees with access to sensitive information. The NRC, in coordination with DOE, has also

developed comprehensive classification guides to protect sensitive nuclear technologies. This ensures that guidance on how to classify different types of information is applied consistently and is well understood.

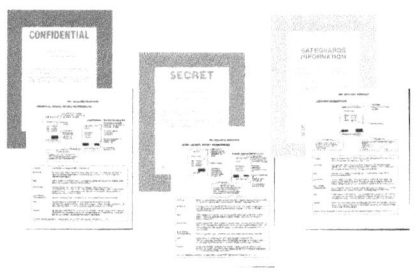

The NRC has a long history of promoting openness and transparency in its regulatory and decision-making processes and is dedicated to appropriately sharing information among organizations and licensees to enhance prevention and response activities to terrorist and other security incidents. However, the NRC remains diligent in controlling sensitive information to prevent unauthorized access to the information by terrorists or other adversaries. Consequently, the NRC continues to balance its commitment to openness with the public with the need to prevent unauthorized releases of sensitive information.

Intelligence

The NRC's intelligence staff assesses threats by reviewing and analyzing intelligence information and routinely communicating with intelligence and law enforcement agencies.

The intelligence staff constantly monitors the domestic and overseas threat environments for credible threats to NRC licensees. The NRC staff also serves as a liaison and coordinator with other organizations and Federal agencies. The NRC ensures that its licensees, its Agreement States, and Federal, State, and local authorities promptly receive notification of any imminent threat or security incident. In addition, the staff annually reviews and briefs the Commission on the current threat environment and any recommended changes to the DBTs based on the evolving characteristics of potential adversaries.

The central mission of the NRC's intelligence staff is to evaluate and warn of possible threats against NRC or Agreement State licensees. Since the 1970s, the NRC has assessed and, in some cases, investigated a variety of threats to licensed nuclear facilities and radioactive materials. These threat assessments provide indications and warnings of potential attacks or other malevolent activities directed at nuclear facilities or radioactive materials licensees. The intelligence staff assesses threats by reviewing thousands of pieces of classified and unclassified message traffic, evaluating intelligence products, and routinely communicating with other intelligence and law enforcement agencies.

In the event of an actual threat, the NRC's intelligence staff forms the core of an interdisciplinary team that assesses the credibility of a communicated threat and, working with NRC physical security counterparts, recommends protective actions to licensees. The NRC's intelligence staff also has a duty officer who is on call 24 hours a day, 7 days a week, to respond to security events and suspicious incidents at NRC-licensed facilities.

To assess and share threat information rapidly, the NRC developed the Information Assessment Team (IAT) process. If the NRC receives information about a possible threat to one of its licensees, it may issue an IAT advisory informing the site. IAT advisories are nonpublic communications from the NRC to licensees that provide information on changes to the threat environment. Another category of advisory, known as a Security Advisory, communicates time sensitive information to help defend against threats directed at NRC-licensed facilities.

Additional interactions involving the intelligence community, DOE, and the IAEA, among others, are conducted in order to keep up-to-date on the latest significant changes to safety and security information. Based on these interactions and information assessments, the NRC informs licensees of changes to the safety environment and threat landscape and interacts with nuclear facilities to improve safety and security accordingly.

Security Programs To Ensure Trustworthiness and Reliability

Access Authorization Programs

The NRC requires licensees to control personnel access to nuclear facilities. Before new employees or contractor employees are allowed unescorted access to the areas containing nuclear and radiological materials they must pass several evaluations and background checks to determine if they are trustworthy and reliable. These evaluations may include drug and alcohol screening, psychological evaluations, prior employment history, and an assessment of education, criminal background (through the FBI), and credit histories.

The NRC continually examines the elements of the access authorization programs. The access authorization requirements employ a graded approach and may include the following depending on the type of nuclear facility :

- additional investigation of individuals who have electronic (cyber) means to adversely impact facility safety, security, or emergency preparedness

- enhanced psychological assessments

- increased information sharing among licensees

- expanded behavioral observation

- reinvestigations of criminal and credit history records for all individuals with unescorted access

- self-reporting of legal actions by individuals with unescorted access

- a 5-year psychological reassessment and a 3-year background reinvestigation for certain critical job functions

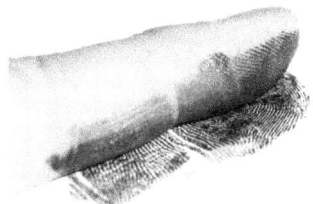

NRC requires fingerprinting for persons with unescorted access to sensitive areas of facilities and information.

Fitness-for-Duty Program

NRC requires licensees that operate certain nuclear facilities to have a fitness-for-duty (FFD) program. The FFD programs provide reasonable assurance that nuclear facility personnel are trustworthy, safe, and will perform their tasks in a reliable manner. This prohibits employees from working while under the influence of any substance, legal or illegal, that may impair their ability to perform their duties, and ensures that they are not mentally or physically impaired to a degree that would adversely affect their ability to safely and competently perform their duties. The NRC requires licensees to conduct random drug and alcohol testing of their employees to detect and deter substance abuse. At least 50 percent of the individuals subject to testing are required to be tested annually. The NRC requires licensees to have procedures to ensure the integrity of the testing process.

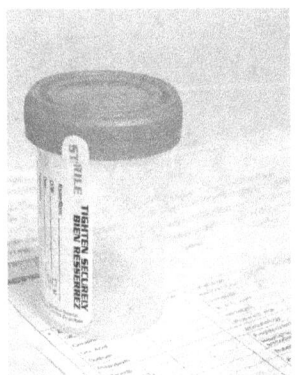

NRC requires drug and alcohol testing of personnel who perform safety-sensitive and security-sensitive work at nuclear power plants and Category I fuel cycle facilities.

The NRC requires licensees to impose work-hour limits on certain workers and to develop procedures to evaluate their fatigue. The NRC fatigue management requirements, published in 2008, limit the work hours of personnel at certain nuclear facilities. The regulations also require a process for persons to report if they are fatigued and prevent licensees from retaliating against those individuals who self-report fatigue. Licensees are also required to conduct a documented fatigue assessment if, among other things, individuals report that they are unfit for work because of fatigue or if workers are observed to be inattentive.

Behavioral Observation Program

The NRC requires certain nuclear facilities to implement a behavioral observation program. This program is conducted by personnel within a facility who are trained specifically on behavioral observation techniques. The program looks for individual behavioral changes that could indicate that a person might act in a manner detrimental to public safety if unmonitored or left unaddressed. Employees are offered counseling if they have job performance problems or exhibit unusual behavior. Similarly, anyone who appears to be under the influence of drugs or alcohol is immediately removed from the work area for evaluation under the licensee's FFD program.

Insider Mitigation Program

The insider mitigation program contains elements of the access authorization, FFD, and behavioral observation programs at certain nuclear facilities. The insider mitigation program helps ensure that those who have unescorted access within a nuclear facility do not pose a potential insider threat. An insider threat is a person who could use the knowledge or access gained by his or her job at a nuclear facility to cause damage or sabotage or potentially aid an adversary. These programs are essential to the overall security of certain nuclear facilities.

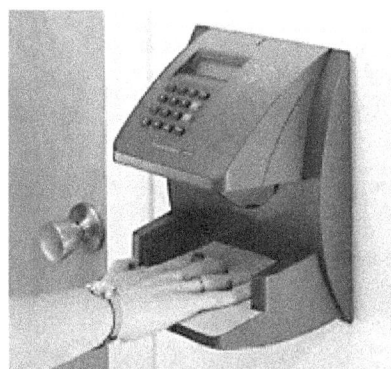

Many licensees use biometrics as part of their access requirements.

International Safety and Security

In 2003, the NRC staff joined with international and domestic partners to discuss with manufacturers of radioactive sources and devices possible ways to make high-risk radioactive sources more secure and less vulnerable to use by persons with malicious intent. The NRC also met with manufacturers to discuss improved methods for use in verifying the legitimacy of purchases of radioactive sources to ensure that these sources are only given to authorized users. Discussions also addressed concerns for ensuring the safe return and disposal of spent radioactive sources.

The U.S. Government made a commitment to implement the IAEA Code of Conduct for the Safety and Security of Radioactive Sources (the Code) and its associated Guidance on Import and Export (the Guidance). In line with the commitments, the NRC considered the provisions of this Code and Guidance in its domestic regulations governing use, transfer, and tracking of the 16 radionuclides of concern. These particular radionuclides of concern are at the highest risk of use by a terrorist. Strong international support for the provisions in the Code and the Guidance is highlighted by the 115 countries that have agreed to implement the Code and 79 that have agreed to implement the Guidance (as of January 2013).

In 2005 and 2010, the NRC implemented rules with enhanced controls over the import and export of radioactive sources. Under the amendments, licensees must apply for specific licenses to export certain radioactive sources listed in Title 10 of the Code of Federal Regulations (10 CFR) Part 110, "Export and Import of Nuclear

Equipment and Material," Appendix P, "Category 1 and 2 Radioactive Material," which includes the high-risk radioactive sources contained in the Code. Licensees are also required to document that the end user is authorized to receive and possess the material and must provide prior notice of shipments. For the export of high-risk sources, the NRC assesses and makes a determination on whether the importing country's regulatory infrastructure is sufficient to maintain adequate control over the material. In countries without adequate regulatory controls, the Code provides for "exceptional circumstances" under which high risk sources can be exported with additional conditions imposed on the licensee.

Chairman Allison M. Macfarlane speaks at the International Atomic Energy Agency.

The NRC regulations in part 110 also address criteria for physical security measures. NRC regulations in 10 CFR Part 110 state that physical security measures in recipient countries must provide protection at least

comparable to the recommendations in the current version of IAEA publication INFCIRC/225, "The Physical Protection of Nuclear Material and Nuclear Facilities."

To support the reviews and to exchange information on best security practices, NRC staff participates in U.S. interagency bilateral physical protection visits to foreign countries possessing special nuclear materials carrying U.S. obligations. The NRC also hosts meetings and tours to demonstrate U.S. physical protection practices. Additionally, the NRC, in partnership with other U.S. agencies, works to strengthen the international physical protection framework by providing technical expert support to the IAEA and by supporting U.S. policy initiatives to secure nuclear materials worldwide.

The NRC continues to support the development of international standards for implementing the recommendations of the IAEA Code of Conduct for the import and export of radioactive sources. This guidance is intended to balance the needs of international cooperation and commerce without affecting safety and security.

CONCLUSION

Protecting the Nation's nuclear facilities and materials is a top priority of the NRC. The NRC works aggressively to protect the public health and safety, promote the common defense and security, and protect the environment by regulating the commercial nuclear industry. Working closely with its partners, the NRC will continue to remain vigilant and provide oversight of security and emergency preparedness activities at nuclear facilities.

NRC Chairman Allison M. Macfarlane and her Commission colleagues are routinely briefed by agency staff.

GLOSSARY

Agreement State

A State that has signed an agreement with the U.S. NRC under which the State regulates the use of byproduct, source, and small quantities of special nuclear material in that State.

Category I Fuel Cycle Facilities

Fuel cycle facilities that possess more than 5,000 grams (about 11 pounds) of strategic special nuclear material (defined as a "formula quantity") or more as computed by the formula, grams = (grams contained U-235) + 2.5 (grams U-233 + grams plutonium).

Classified Information

The two primary types of classified information at the NRC and NRC-regulated facilities are:

1. National Security Information (NSI): Information classified by an Executive Order, whose compromise would cause some degree of damage to national security.

2. Restricted Data (RD): Information classified by the Atomic Energy Act of 1954, as amended, whose compromise would assist in the design, manufacture, or use of nuclear weapons.

The lowest level of classified information is Confidential; the next higher is Secret, and the highest is Top Secret. Confidential, Secret, and Top Secret information will also be either NSI or RD. Access to classified information requires a need-to-know and a personnel security clearance equal to or higher than the level of information.

Depleted Uranium

Source material uranium in which the isotope uranium-235 is less than 0.711 weight percent of the total uranium present. Depleted uranium does not include special nuclear material.

Design Basis Threat

A profile of the type, composition, and capabilities of a possible adversary. The NRC and certain licensees use the DBT as a basis for designing safeguards systems to protect against acts of radiological sabotage and to prevent the theft of special nuclear material. This term is applied to clearly identify for a licensee the expected capability of its facility to withstand a threat.

Emergency Preparedness

Action taken to be ready for emergencies before they happen. The objective of emergency preparedness is to simplify decision-making during emergencies. The emergency preparedness process incorporates the means to rapidly identify, evaluate, categorize, and react to a wide spectrum of emergency conditions.

Hostile Action

An act toward a nuclear power plant or radioactive material facility or its personnel that includes the use of force to destroy equipment, take hostages, or intimidate the licensee to achieve an end. This covers an attack by air, land, or water that uses guns, explosives, projectiles, vehicles, or other devices to deliver destructive force. Other acts that satisfy the overall intent may be incorporated.

Licensed Material

Source material, special nuclear material, or byproduct material received, possessed, used, transferred, or disposed of under a general or specific license issued by the NRC.

Licensee

An entity or individual authorized by the NRC to conduct the following activities:

- constructing, operating, and decommissioning commercial reactors and fuel cycle facilities

- possessing, using, processing, exporting, importing, and certain aspects of transporting nuclear materials and waste

- siting, designing, constructing, operating, and closing waste disposal sites

Nonpower Reactor

Nuclear reactors primarily used for research, training, and development. Formerly referred to as research and test reactors.

NRC Headquarters Operations Center

The NRC HOC is located in Rockville, MD, and serves as the focal coordination point for communicating with NRC licensees, State agencies, and other Federal agencies about operating events in both the nuclear reactor and nuclear materials industry. Headquarters operations officers, who are trained to receive, evaluate, and respond to reported events, staff the HOC 24 hours a day, 7 days a week.

Nuclear Energy

The energy liberated by a nuclear reaction (fission or fusion) or by radioactive decay.

Nuclear Power Plant

An electrical generating facility that uses a nuclear reactor as its heat source to provide steam to a turbine generator.

Nuclear Waste

A particular type of radioactive waste that is produced as part of the nuclear fuel cycle (i.e., those activities needed to produce nuclear fission or the splitting of the atom). These activities include the extraction of uranium from ore, the concentration of the extracted uranium, the processing of the concentrated uranium into nuclear fuel, and the disposal of byproducts. "Radioactive waste" is a broader term that includes all waste that contains radioactivity. Residues from water treatment, contaminated equipment from oil drilling, and tailings from the processing of metals such as vanadium and copper also contain radioactivity but are not "nuclear waste" because they are produced outside of the nuclear fuel cycle. The NRC generally regulates only those wastes produced in the nuclear fuel cycle (e.g., uranium mill tailings, depleted uranium, and spent fuel rods).

Radionuclide

An unstable isotope of an element that emits radiation as it decays or disintegrates spontaneously.

Safeguards

The use of material control and accounting programs, physical protection equipment, and security forces to verify that all special nuclear material is properly controlled and accounted for. As used by the IAEA, "safeguards" refers to verification that the "peaceful use" commitments made in binding nonproliferation agreements, both bilateral and multilateral, are honored.

Safeguards Information

A special category of sensitive unclassified information authorized to be protected under Section 147 of the Atomic Energy Act of 1954, as amended. SGI concerns the physical protection of operating power reactors, spent fuel shipments, strategic special nuclear material, or other radioactive material.

While SGI is considered to be sensitive unclassified information, its handling and protection more closely resemble the handling of classified Confidential information rather than other sensitive unclassified information.

The categories of individuals who are permitted access to SGI are listed in 10 CFR 73.21, "Protection of Safeguards Information: Performance Requirements," 10 CFR 73.22, "Protection of Safeguards Information: Specific Requirements," and 10 CFR 73.23, "Protection of Safeguards Information—Modified Handling: Specific Requirements."

Sensitive Unclassified Nonsafeguards Information

Information that is generally not publicly available, encompassing a wide variety of categories (e.g., personnel privacy, attorney-client privilege, investigations information, confidential source).

Under 10 CFR 2.390, "Public Inspections, Exemptions, Requests for Withholding," information about a licensee's or applicant's physical protection or material control and accounting program for special nuclear material not otherwise designated as SGI or classified as National Security Information or Restricted Data must be protected in the same manner as commercial or financial information. In other words, such information is exempt from public disclosure. Policy and procedures related to sensitive unclassified non-safeguards information are the responsibility of the NRC Office of Information Services.

Special Nuclear Material

Plutonium, uranium-233, or uranium enriched in the uranium-235 isotope.

Spent Fuel Pool

An underwater storage and cooling facility for spent (used) fuel elements that have been removed from a reactor.

Spent Nuclear Fuel

Fuel that has been withdrawn from a nuclear reactor following irradiation, has undergone at least one year's decay since being used as a source of energy in a power reactor, and has not been chemically separated into its constituent elements by reprocessing. Spent fuel includes the special nuclear material, byproduct material, source material, and other radioactive materials associated with fuel assemblies.

LIST OF ACRONYMS

CFR	Code of Federal Regulations
COOP	Continuity of Operations
CSD	Cyber Security Directorate
DBT	Design Basis Threat
DHS	U.S. Department of Homeland Security
DOE	U.S. Department of Energy
FBI	Federal Bureau of Investigations
FFD	Fitness-for-Duty
FEMA	Federal Emergency Management Agency
HAB	Hostile Action-Based
HOC	Headquarters Operations Center
IAEA	International Atomic Energy Agency
IAT	Information Assessment Team
ISFSI	Independent Spent Fuel Storage Installation
LVS	License Verification System
NIPP	National Infrastructure Protection Plan
NORAD	North American Aerospace Defense Command
NPR	Nonpower Reactor
NRC	U.S. Nuclear Regulatory Commission
NRF	National Response Framework
NSI	National Security Information
NSTS	National Source Tracking System
RD	Restricted Data
SGI	Safeguards Information
WBL	Web-Based Licensing

NUREG/BR-0314, Rev. 3

October 2013

www.ingramcontent.com/pod-product-compliance
Lightning Source LLC
Chambersburg PA
CBHW080346290526
45791CB00009BA/2755